KT-163-344

A TASTE OF BRITAIN

Roz Denny

Wayland

Titles in this series

A TASTE OF

Britain	Italy
The Caribbean	Japan
China	Mexico
France	Spain
India	West Africa

Cover *Tower Bridge is a historic landmark on the River Thames in London.*

Frontispiece *Buttered scones with jam, and a cup of strongish tea with milk, make a traditional British afternoon tea – a light meal eaten at about 4 pm.*

Editor: Anna Girling
Designer: Jean Wheeler

First published in 1994 by
Wayland (Publishers) Ltd
61 Western Road, Hove
East Sussex, BN3 1JD, England

British Library Cataloguing in Publication Data
Denny, Roz
Taste of Britain. – (Food Around the
World Series)
I. Title II. Series
641.0941

ISBN 0 7502 0797 3

Typeset by Dorchester Typesetting Group Ltd
Printed and bound by Lego, Italy

Contents

'Good, plain cooking'

'Good, plain cooking.' That is how people in Britain like to describe their food. But many foreign visitors to Britain think British food is boring and often badly cooked. So what is the truth?

Britain is a very rich agricultural country. There is excellent grass for animals to graze on, top-quality crops grow plentifully, and farming is extremely efficient. So British cooks have not felt the need to cook rich, elaborate dishes because the foods were naturally full of flavour. British cookery is based on farmhouse dishes, such as roast meats, pies, cakes, jams, pickles –

Roast beef with vegetables. Excellent fresh produce, simply cooked, brings out the best in British cooking.

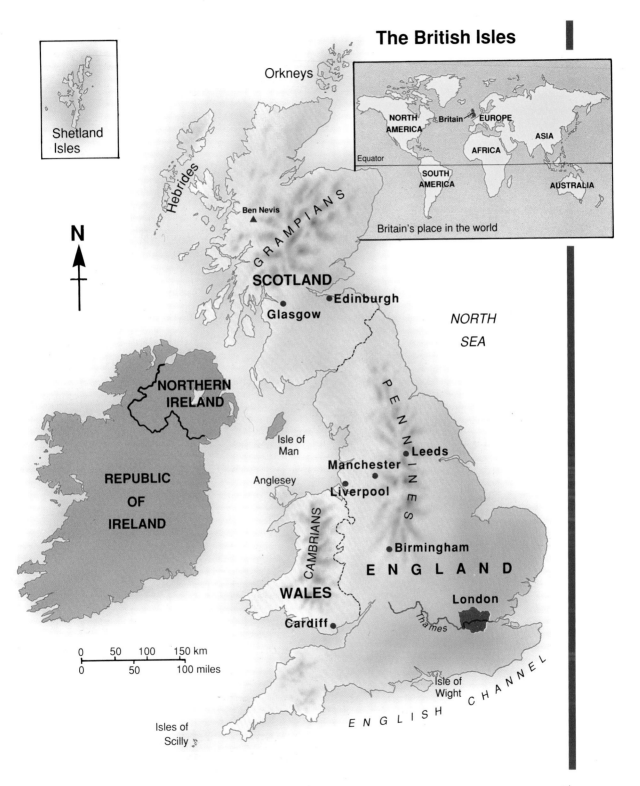

The British Isles

Orkneys

Shetland Isles

NORTH AMERICA — Britain — EUROPE

AFRICA — ASIA

Equator

SOUTH AMERICA

AUSTRALIA

Britain's place in the world

Hebrides

N

G R A M P I A N S

Ben Nevis

SCOTLAND

● Edinburgh

● Glasgow

NORTH SEA

NORTHERN IRELAND

REPUBLIC OF IRELAND

Isle of Man

Anglesey

P E N N I N E S

● Leeds

Manchester ●

Liverpool ●

C A M B R I A N S

● Birmingham

E N G L A N D

WALES

London

Cardiff ●

Thames

0   50   100   150 km

0   50   100 miles

Isle of Wight

E N G L I S H   C H A N N E L

Isles of Scilly

5

A taste of Britain

and, above all, wonderful puddings. Unfortunately for many visitors to Britain, however, such good cooking is often only available in people's homes, so few of them get to eat really tasty, traditional British food.

Britain is not just home to traditional, plain cooking. It was once the centre of a large empire, covering many countries and lasting from the mid-eighteenth century through to the 1950s. Britain has welcomed people from these other countries to live and work. They in turn have brought their own dishes and foods, many of which have become firm British favourites, especially dishes from India, Pakistan, Bangladesh, Cyprus, the West Indies, Africa and Hong Kong. So, while we may talk about traditional British foods, in fact the normal British foods eaten today are those of a modern, multicultural society.

British society today is a mixture of people whose families have come from many parts of the world. The mix of different traditions has introduced delicious new foods to Britain.

The land and farming

Compared to many countries, Britain is a very small island (it has an area of less than 250,000 sq km) yet it is home to around 54 million people. Britain is the main island of the British Isles, the other being Ireland, to the west. It is situated off the west coast of northern Europe and is separated from Europe by a shallow sea, called the North Sea.

Britain actually consists of three countries – England, Scotland and Wales. England is the biggest. Scotland lies to the north and Wales to the west. The Welsh and Scottish peoples are very proud of their 'differentness' and any foreign visitor mistaking them for English will be quickly corrected.

The British capital is London. It has a population of over 6 million people and is one of the biggest cities in the world. Other important cities include Birmingham, Leeds, Manchester and Liverpool, Cardiff in Wales and Glasgow and Edinburgh in Scotland.

Edinburgh, the capital of Scotland, is an ancient city with many old buildings.

A taste of Britain

Above *Purple, flowering heather on a Yorkshire moor.* Below *Ben Nevis reaches 1,343 m above sea level.*

The countryside and climate

Britain is a mixture of different landscapes. There are gently rolling hills; wide, flat plains; wild, craggy moors; and mountain ranges which, although quite low compared to elsewhere in the world, nevertheless look quite impressive.

The main mountain ranges are the Pennines (known as the backbone of England because they run up the centre of the country); the Cambrians in Wales; and the Grampians in Scotland, containing Britain's highest mountain, Ben Nevis. The most famous river is the Thames, which runs through London.

The climate is described as 'temperate' – that is, it is neither too hot nor too cold. The rainfall is generally high and there are few droughts. Foreign visitors (and the British themselves!) often grumble that it rains too much, especially in the summer.

Farming

In Britain the land is fertile and the rainfall good. This means that crops grow well and there is good grazing land for cattle and sheep. The land is quite easy to farm because it is not too rough and stony, and there are many excellent roads for taking produce to markets and shops. British farmers are among some of the best in the world, and use a lot of modern machinery. As more machines are used, fewer and fewer people are needed to work on the land.

Farmers use a lot of modern machinery. Combine harvesters are used to cut cereal crops.

A taste of Britain

Fruit farms produce apples for eating or making into juice or cider.

In general, the south and east of Britain produces cereals and fodder crops including wheat, maize and rape seed. In cooler parts of Britain, particularly Scotland, oats and barley are grown. Barley is used to make the Scottish drink whisky. Across southern England there are fruit farms where apples (for eating or making into cider), strawberries, raspberries and cherries are grown. In the south-west, where the grass is rich, cattle are reared for dairy products and beef. This area is famous for its thick cream and cheeses.

In south-west England, where the rainfall is high, the lush, green grass is ideal for grazing dairy cattle.

In hilly areas, such as in north Wales and Scotland, the land cannot be ploughed for cereals. Here, sheep are reared, both for their wool and their meat.

Sheep are reared on the mountains of Snowdonia, in Wales.

Fishing used to be an important industry all round the coast of Britain. Herrings, mackerel, salmon, haddock and cod were caught and preserved by salting or smoking. This led to specialities such as kippers (smoked herrings) and smoked salmon. Today, most fishing is carried out off the coasts of eastern Scotland and north-east England.

Fishing boats in harbour on the east coast of Scotland.

British food through history

Toad-in-the-hole and (below) *a picture of a pineapple dating from the early 1600s.*

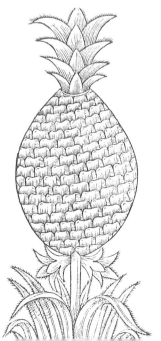

Many traditional British dishes still eaten today have developed from recipes used long ago. These dishes often have unusual, amusing names, whose original meaning is now difficult for us to understand. For example: maids of honour are little sweet tarts; singing hinnies are flat, fruity scones, cooked on a griddle, which seem to sing as they sizzle; toad-in-the-hole consists of sausages cooked in batter in the oven.

During the sixteenth century, many British sailors set off to explore America (not long before this, no one in Europe had known America existed). From the reign of Queen Elizabeth I (1558-1603) onwards, new foods from America, such as tomatoes, potatoes and pineapples, were brought to Britain and grown by farmers in fields and hothouses. Potatoes were to become an essential part of British cooking.

During the late-eighteenth century, British farmers invented many new farming methods and machines. British farming became very efficient.

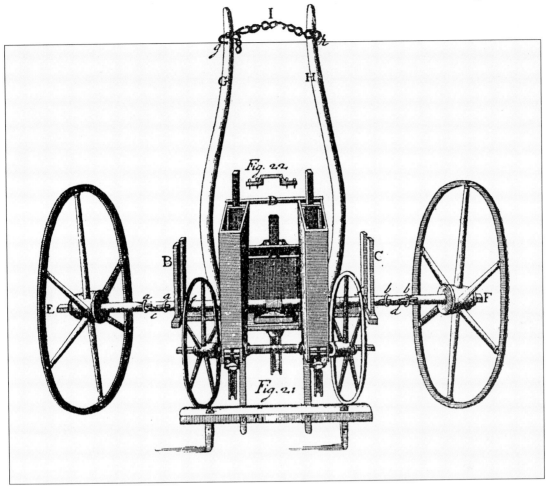

As a result, food was plentiful. Animals could be fed through the winter on fodder crops instead of being killed in the autumn. Fresh milk, cheese, butter and meat became available throughout the winter.

Up until the nineteenth century, many foreign travellers to Britain thought the food served in inns and homes was some of the best in Europe. However, by the reign of Queen Victoria (1837-1901) Britain had become an industrial country. People were encouraged to work hard and make a lot of money.

Jethro Tull was a famous British inventor in the eighteenth century. This is a diagram of his machine for planting seeds.

13

A taste of Britain

In Victorian times, children from well-off families ate in their nursery, away from adults.

These hard-working Victorians believed that plainly cooked food and good table manners were more important than tasty food. The image of poor British food probably dates from this time.

Food in a Tudor kitchen

As an example of British food in the past, we can discover what was eaten by Tudor kings and queens, such as Henry VIII and Elizabeth I, over 400 years ago. Surprisingly, many Tudor dishes would be familiar to British people today. There were great sides of roast beef and roast pork, delicious pies and puddings, fruits, ale (a sort of beer), rich cheeses, butter and cream. Fresh vegetables, unusual salad plants and herbs were grown in the gardens of both rich and poor people. Plants included purslane, corn salad, sorrel, chives, sage and mint.

The royal kitchens were huge and open. Large joints of meat were cooked in front of a roaring fire and turned on a revolving spit by small kitchen boys.

Bread was the staple food for most people. There was a rough brown bread for the poor and better-quality, white bread for the wealthy. Much bread was eaten. In fact, thick slices of bread were used as plates, called trenchers. Leftover bread was always used up and was often made into stuffing for roast meats.

A royal feast in 1491. The noblewoman is eating from a trencher of bread.

Food in Britain today

A stallholder in London selling yams and green bananas – traditional ingredients of Caribbean cooking.

British people today enjoy many dishes and recipes from all over the world. Pasta from Italy, American-style hamburgers and stir-fry dishes from the Far East are now all thought to be normal everyday food.

In particular, dishes from Asia and the Caribbean have become very popular. Britain has had links with these places since the days of its empire. In the 1950s and 1960s many people from the Caribbean, India and Pakistan came to live and work in Britain, bringing their own styles of cooking with them. Indian-style curries, for example, are now eaten in many homes, as well as traditional

A family enjoying traditional Asian snack food.

British dishes such as shepherd's pie and fish and chips. In fact, sometimes, British people mix the two types of food together – curry and chips, for example!

Another trend in British eating is vegetarianism. The British have always shown concern for animals. Many are now becoming vegetarians, particularly young people. Supermarkets now sell more and more foods that are free of animal produce and schools offer vegetarian choices at lunch time.

This graph shows how the number of vegetarians in Britain has increased in recent years. The number of people who do not eat red meat (beef and lamb, for example) has grown even more quickly. (Source: The Vegetarian Society.)

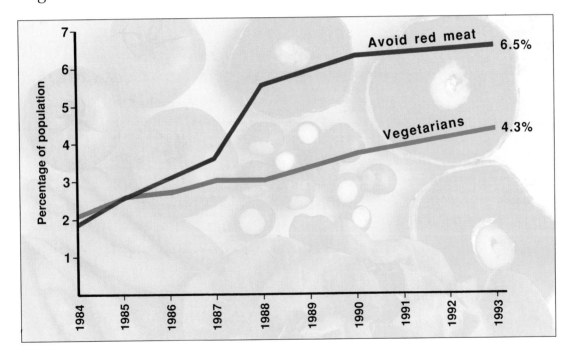

Shopping

Traditionally, food is bought from individual shops – butchers, greengrocers, fishmongers and bakers. Some towns have markets selling fresh produce, often home-grown.

Today, however, more and more food shopping is done in large super-markets built on the edges of town. Many dishes are sold ready-cooked, either fresh or frozen, and only need to be reheated (more than half of all British homes have a microwave oven, which can be used for reheating food). In many British families both parents go out to work, and ready-cooked meals are quick and easy.

Many pubs are hundreds of years old. They always have a name. This one is called the 'Rose and Crown'.

Eating out

No British town or village is complete without at least one public house (or pub, for short). These are inns serving drinks such as beer, wine and spirits. Pubs provide a warm, relaxed atmosphere where people can meet and chat. Many serve cheap 'pub grub', especially at lunch time. Typical food might be sandwiches, pies or a ploughman's lunch (see page 28).

In addition, there are a great many restaurants. Usually, these specialize in dishes from a foreign country – for example from India, Thailand, Italy or the USA.

British people often like to buy hot, ready-cooked food from shops called 'takeaways'. These do a roaring trade in chips, so they are sometimes nicknamed 'chippies'. The most traditional are fish-and-chip shops, selling fresh fish that has been dipped in batter and fried until crisp, served with thick-cut chips.

Fish and chips from the fish-and-chip shop – a famous British tradition.

Meal times

Meal times in Britain can cause some confusion – even among the British! The type of meal, the time, and what it is called, all vary in different parts of the country. Even more confusingly, the same word can be used to describe very different meals.

The main meal is generally called dinner, and this can be in the early evening or in the middle of the day (the midday meal may also be called lunch). Typical main meals are grilled meat, chops, sausages, fried fish or a stew.

A typical main meal which might be eaten at home, at a café or in a canteen: fish with potatoes and peas, served with bread and butter and a cup of tea.

An example of high tea in Scotland: bread and butter, cold meat, salad, scones, pie and fruit cake.

School dinner usually consists of a hot main course of meat or fish, with potatoes and vegetables, followed by pudding.

These will usually be served with potatoes and other vegetables.

In the industrial north, where many people traditionally worked in factories or mines, the main meal is served at about 6 pm. This is when the workers would return home tired and hungry after work. In some parts of Britain this main meal is called high tea, or simply tea. There is meat, fish or pie, with vegetables and bread and butter, followed by pudding or cakes. To drink there is tea or beer. Then, before bedtime there is another, light meal, called supper. This is eaten at about 10 pm and may consist of cheese and biscuits, fruit cake or even a quick meal from the local takeaway.

In other parts of Britain, mostly in the south, the main meal is at lunch time, at around 1 pm. However, this is becoming less popular as more people work some distance from home. Many people now eat a quick sandwich or other snack in the middle of the day and have a hot main meal at about 7 pm. Many people call *this* main evening meal supper.

School meals

Most British schoolchildren eat lunch at school in the middle of the day. This may be a hot meal provided by the school, or children may bring their own cold lunch, called a 'packed lunch', consisting of sandwiches, crisps, fruit

and a drink. The hot meals are called school dinners and usually offer a choice of meat, fish or salad meals, plus a pudding or fruit.

Breakfast

As in many other parts of the world, British people mostly eat a light breakfast of cereals, toast and marmalade and tea or coffee. Traditionally, however, Britain is famous for magnificent and large cooked breakfasts. Nowadays, people may only eat a cooked breakfast at weekends. The meal will start with fresh grapefruit or fruit juice, followed by a plate of fried food such as bacon, sausages, egg, tomato, black pudding (see page 26) and a crisp, golden slice of fried bread.

Many schoolchildren take a packed lunch to school

A full English fried breakfast.

A taste of Britain

In Scotland (and elsewhere in Britain when the weather is cold), porridge is popular at breakfast time. It is a thick mixture of oats, milk and water and is a warm way to start the day.

Sunday lunch

Sunday lunch is a popular time for family and friends to get together and enjoy a large meal. The main course will be a roast joint of meat, such as beef, lamb, pork or chicken, served with roast potatoes, boiled vegetables and gravy (a light sauce made with the juices from the meat). In many parts of Britain, roast beef is accompanied by little crispy puffs of batter, called Yorkshire puddings. The main course is followed by a sweet pudding, such as apple pie or trifle.

This family is enjoying Sunday lunch of roast beef and Yorkshire pudding.

Afternoon tea

This a very British meal! It is thought to have been started as a fashion by the Duchess of Bedford in 1840. The Duchess got hungry between lunch, served at midday, and dinner in the evening, so she had tea at about 4 pm. The main part of the meal is a pot of freshly brewed tea, served with milk and sugar or slices of lemon. Then there are plates of thinly cut bread and butter; sandwiches of cucumber, egg or tomato; buttered scones with jam; and pieces of sponge cake or fruit cake.

Traditional afternoon tea can be rather dainty! This one consists of small, neat sandwiches, scones with cream and jam, cake – and of course tea.

Specialities and regional foods

Pies and pasties

Cold meat pies are made with pork, ham or veal wrapped in a crisp, rich pastry called hot watercrust pastry. The meat is finely chopped and put inside the pastry raw. When cooked and cooled, the meat is solid and the pie easy to cut into slices. These pies are popular for picnics and packed lunches.

Pork pie is cut into thick slices.

There are also hot pies, of which the most famous is steak and kidney pie. Chunks of beef and kidney are stewed in a tasty gravy, then put into a pie dish, topped with pastry and baked.

Other pastries are called pasties. The most famous are from Cornwall, in the south-west and are called Cornish pasties. These individual pies are half-moon-shaped envelopes of pastry, filled with minced beef, potato and onion. In the past, pasties were a good way for people to take a large snack to work with them, to eat in the middle of the day. In the town of Luton people ate a pasty that contained meat at one end and apple at the other. In this way, they could eat a meat course and pudding in one go!

A crisp, rich pastry, called shortcrust, is used to make Cornish pasties.

Stews

Stews and casseroles are dishes of meat, such as beef, pork or chicken, plus lots of vegetables, cooked slowly in stock or gravy in the oven until the meat is tender. Lancashire hot pot is a popular dish from the north of England. This is a stew topped with slices of potato which turn golden and crispy when baked in the oven.

In the past, to make a little meat stretch to feed large, hungry families, cooks would make little dumplings of flour and suet. These would be placed on top of the bubbling stew for the last half-hour of cooking.

Lancashire hot pot is a meat stew topped with slices of potato.

A taste of Britain

British 'bangers' are usually small and fat and served hot.

A Scottish butcher selling haggis.

Sausages

Sausages in Britain are quite different from those in the rest of Europe. They are made of fresh meat, usually minced pork, mixed with breadcrumbs and spices. There are many different types from different regions. The British are very fond of sausages, which they call 'bangers'. They are either fried or grilled. Sausages can be served for breakfast with eggs, bacon and tomatoes, or as a main meal with mashed potatoes or chips and vegetables.

Other sausages are made with offal. One of these is called black pudding, eaten mostly in the north of England. It is a sausage made of pig's blood mixed with breadcrumbs and spices.

A speciality from Scotland is called haggis. This is a mixture of offal, oatmeal, onion and spices, stuffed into a sheep's stomach. It is boiled and usually served with mashed turnips.

Cheeses

Most of Britain's cheeses are hard and made from cow's milk. Many have been made for hundreds of years.

There are nine main types of British cheese. Most have regional names, such as Red Leicester, Caerphilly, Cheshire, Stilton and so on, but they can also be made in other counties. One of them, Cheddar, is perhaps the most imitated cheese in the world, with versions made

British cheeses are usually made in large cylinder shapes, called truckles, from which triangular wedges are cut.

in other countries such as New Zealand, Canada, Australia and Ireland.

Bread

If it is well made by local bakers, British bread can be among the best in the world – light, crusty and full of flavour. Unfortunately, much of the bread sold in Britain is mass-produced and is sold ready-sliced in plastic bags.

In recent years, however, supermarkets and shops have been selling breads made to old recipes.

British bakers also sell simple but delicious buns and cakes. Hot cross buns, marked with a cross, are eaten at Easter; scones are plain buns, split open and buttered; Eccles cakes are round parcels of pastry filled with dried fruit.

A ploughman's lunch

A ploughman's lunch is a light meal often served in pubs. It is basically bread, cheese and pickles. It is very easy to do yourself.

Cut some British cheeses, such as Cheddar, Stilton, Cheshire or Red Leicester, into wedges. Allow about 125 g of cheese per person. Lay on a plate with chunks of crusty bread, some pickled onions, chutney, a fresh tomato and some lettuce.

British puddings

The British generally call the sweet course pudding. Some of the best British recipes are for puddings. Many have wonderful, funny names such as trifle, brown betty, spotted dick, fool, crumble, roly-poly and so on. Puddings are often served with custard, a thick sauce of milk, eggs and sugar, flavoured with vanilla.

   Here is a list of popular puddings.

Trifle This is a cold pudding consisting of pieces of cake soaked in sherry or fruit juice, layered with fresh fruit, sometimes topped with jelly, and the whole covered with whipped cream.

Fool Another cold pudding, made by mixing whipped cream with custard and adding stewed fruit such as gooseberries or rhubarb.

Crumble A hot pudding with a fruit base, such as chopped apples, blackberries or gooseberries, topped with a crumbly mixture of flour, butter and sugar.

Roly-poly This hot pudding consists of a strip of suet pastry, spread with jam or

Rhubarb fool is a smooth mixture of cream, custard and stewed fruit.

A taste of Britain

Summer pudding is made by lining a pudding basin with bread and filling it with lightly cooked juicy fruits, such as raspberries and redcurrants. The pudding is left to chill in the fridge until the juice has soaked through the bread. It can then be turned out on to a plate.

fruit and rolled up like a swiss roll. It is then baked in the oven.

Syllabub This is one of Britain's oldest puddings. In Tudor times it was made of wine mixed with fresh milk flavoured with sugar and spices. King Charles II, who ruled from 1660 to 1685, is said to have milked cows in St. James's Park, London, straight into his glass of red wine. Nowadays, syllabub is made by mixing whipped cream with sugar, lemon and, sometimes, sherry.

Pancakes Light, hot, thin rounds of fried batter, made from eggs, flour and milk. In Britain, Shrove Tuesday is also called Pancake Day. This is the day before Lent, which is a period of fasting for Christians. The idea was that you used up foods such as eggs and flour before starting to fast. On Pancake Day, people have fun cooking pancakes, tossing them in the air and catching them in the pan to cook both sides.

Treacle tart This is a pastry tart base filled with golden syrup (which used to be called treacle), breadcrumbs, grated lemon rind and ground ginger.

Treacle tart is sweet and sticky.

Food from gardens and allotments

The British are very keen gardeners. Many people like to grow their own fresh vegetables and fruits, such as potatoes, runner beans, apples and raspberries. In towns, where gardens may be small, gardeners can pay to use a small plot of land, called an allotment, owned by the local council.

Nowadays, many fruit farmers grow soft fruits, such as strawberries, and allow people to pick the fruit for themselves. These are called 'pick your own' farms, and they are very popular.

With so much fresh produce in the summer months, the British have developed ways of preserving fruit and vegetables to last through the winter. There are all kinds of delicious jams, jellies (clear jams), pickles and chutneys.

Above *Allotments are used for growing vegetables.*
Below *A day out at a pick-your-own farm.*

Jams and jellies
Jams are made by boiling fruit with sugar until they set (become firm, not

31

runny). Jellies are made in the same way, but use only the juice of the fruit. Popular jams are made of strawberries, raspberries and plums. One of the most popular fruit preserves is marmalade. This is a chunky, bittersweet, orange jam and it is eaten on toast for breakfast.

Jams are spread on toast and scones (see photograph on title page) and used to sandwich layers of sponge cake together. They are also spooned into small pastry tarts. Jellies are often eaten with meat – redcurrant jelly with lamb, for example.

Fruit curds, such as lemon curd, are another way of preserving fruit. Curds are like thick custards and are made of fruit pulp or juice, cooked with eggs, butter and sugar until thickened.

Pickles and chutneys

Pickles are prepared vegetables, such as baby onions, cucumbers and cauliflower, preserved in vinegar and spices. After pickling, the vegetables have a strong, tangy flavour. They are served with cold meats and cheeses.

Chutneys came from India and were introduced in Britain in the nineteenth century. They are mixtures of chopped fruits and vegetables, such as apples, mangoes, tomatoes and onions, cooked with sugar, vinegar and spices.

A jar of pickled onions.

A British Christmas

The Christian festival of Christmas, which celebrates the birth of Jesus Christ, is the main public holiday in Britain. Many offices and factories close for up to two weeks, from the afternoon of Christmas Eve (24 December) until after New Year's Day (1 January). The days before Christmas are a time for parties and going out with friends. On Christmas Day itself (25 December) families get together to exchange presents – and eat!

The traditional Christmas still celebrated today started in Victorian times in the nineteenth century. The main meal is eaten in the middle of the day or early evening. After much preparation in the kitchen, all the family sits down together to eat. The table is laid with candles and holly and each person is given a cracker to pull.

The centrepiece of the meal is a roasted turkey. This is

For Christmas lunch, roast turkey is served with roast potatoes, vegetables and cranberry sauce (bottom left).

A taste of Britain

Flaming brandy gives a special flavour to rich, dark Christmas pudding.

Mince pies are filled with mincemeat. In the past, mincemeat really did have minced meat in it!

served with lots of accompaniments, such as roast potatoes, Brussels sprouts, chestnuts, thin sausages, bacon rolls and a tasty mixture called stuffing, made of breadcrumbs, onions and herbs and cooked 'stuffed' inside the turkey. For sauces, there will be cranberry sauce, a creamy white sauce called bread sauce, and gravy.

For dessert there is a magnificent, hot, steamed pudding, called Christmas pudding. This is made to a very old recipe dating back hundreds of years. It consists of breadcrumbs, sugar, rich dried fruits such as raisins and sultanas, nuts, spices and suet. The pudding is usually made about six weeks before Christmas. Today, many people buy ready-made puddings from shops and supermarkets. The Christmas pudding is brought to the table with great ceremony – brandy is poured over it and set alight, to great cheers from the family.

Other Christmas treats are mince pies. These are small tarts filled with a dried-fruit mixture called mincemeat. In the past, this mixture really did have minced beef in it, as well as fruits, spices and sugar. Sometimes, people also like to have a rich fruit cake, covered in marzipan and sweet white icing, to eat on Christmas afternoon.

Shepherd's pie

This is a popular mid-week meal with a tasty, meaty filling and creamy potato topping. Traditionally, the meat used would have been leftover lamb or beef from the Sunday roast, so this dish was often served on Mondays. Nowadays, fresh meat may be used, so it can be dished up on any day of the week.

Equipment

two saucepans
large wooden spoon
small knife and
    chopping board
large pie dish
measuring jug
colander
potato masher
fork

Shepherd's pie is a warm, filling meal.

35

A taste of Britain

Ingredients
Serves 4

500 g fresh beef or lamb mince

2-3 tablespoons sunflower oil

1 onion, peeled and chopped

2 medium carrots, peeled and chopped

600 ml stock (make this by putting a stock cube in boiling water)

1 teaspoon dried, mixed herbs,

1 tablespoon Worcestershire sauce (if you like)

1 kg potatoes, peeled and halved

knob of butter or low-fat spread

a little milk

salt and ground black pepper

1 Fry the meat in the oil in one of the saucepans until browned, stirring well with the wooden spoon to break up any lumps.

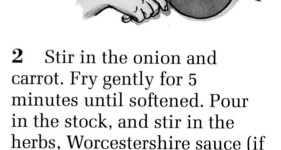

2 Stir in the onion and carrot. Fry gently for 5 minutes until softened. Pour in the stock, and stir in the herbs, Worcestershire sauce (if using), salt and pepper.

3 Bring to the boil, then turn down the heat and cook, without a lid on, for about 20 minutes, stirring occasionally. Cool and pour into a pie dish.

4 Meanwhile, boil the potatoes in another saucepan in plenty of water for about 15 minutes or until just tender. Test them by sticking in a knife – if it goes in easily the potatoes are cooked. Carefully drain off the water through a colander in the sink.

Always be careful in the kitchen. Hot oil and boiling liquid can burn. A hot grill can be dangerous. Ask an adult to help you.

6 Spoon the potato on to the meat and spread over the top with the back of a fork.

5 Return the potatoes to the pan and mash with the masher, making sure you get rid of all the lumps. Stir in the butter or spread and enough milk to make the potatoes soft but not runny. Add salt and pepper.

7 Heat your grill until it is quite hot. Put the pie under the grill and brown the top until golden and bubbling. Serve with freshly boiled cabbage or sprouts.

Bubble and squeak

Ingredients
Serves 6

1 onion, peeled and chopped
2 tablespoons sunflower oil, plus extra if needed
about 500 g cooked potato, mashed
about 500 g cold cooked cabbage
a little grated nutmeg
salt and ground black pepper

Equipment

knife and chopping board
frying pan
mixing bowl and spoon
fish slice
kitchen paper towel

This is a breakfast dish using up leftover vegetables. It is thought of as a cockney dish (cockneys are people born and brought up in the East End of London). It is often served with fried eggs, bacon and sausages. If you are vegetarian, serve it with grilled mushrooms and tomatoes instead. This dish really does bubble and squeak as it cooks!

Bubble and squeak (bottom).

1 Fry the onion in the oil in a frying pan for about 5 minutes until just softened. Remove and mix into the cold, mashed potato.

2 Cut the cabbage into thin strips and mix into the potato. Add salt, pepper and a pinch or two of nutmeg.

3 Shape the mixture into 6 little cakes with your hands. It may help to wet your hands in cold water first. Place the cakes on a plate. Heat up some more oil in the frying pan.

4 When the oil is quite hot, carefully slip the cakes into the pan using the fish slice. Fry gently on each side for about 3-5 minutes until browned, golden and crisp.

5 Put on a plate covered with kitchen paper towel. This will soak up any excess oil. Serve warm with other breakfast foods.

Welsh rarebit

Ingredients
Serves 4

150 g cheese (e.g.
    Cheddar, Red
    Leicester or
    Caerphilly)
butter
2 tablespoons milk
ground black pepper
mustard powder
4 slices bread

Equipment

grater
saucepan
tablespoon
wooden spoon
oven gloves

The word 'supper' means different things in different parts of Britain. Sometimes it means a light meal before bedtime, sometimes it means a full-size meal at about 7 pm. A popular light supper dish is Welsh rarebit.

Welsh rarebit is an easy-to-make snack.

1 Grate the cheese on the largest holes on the grater.

2 Melt a big knob of butter in a saucepan with two tablespoons of milk. Add the cheese, pepper and a pinch of mustard.

3 Melt carefully until thickened, stirring with a wooden spoon. Do not let it boil. Keep the mixture warm.

Always be careful when using a hot grill. Wear oven gloves. Ask an adult to help you.

4 Heat your grill and toast the bread.

5 Spread the cheese mixture on the toast. Return to the grill and cook until lightly browned and bubbling. Serve straight away. Eat with a knife and fork.

Apple crumble

Ingredients
Serves 4-6

180 g plain white
    flour, or 90 g
    wholemeal flour
    and 90 g plain
    white flour
90 g butter or
    margarine, chilled
about 5 tablespoons
    caster sugar
750 g cooking
    apples, e.g.
    Bramleys or
    Granny Smiths
½ teaspoon ground
    cinnamon
1 tablespoon
    demerara sugar

Equipment

large mixing bowl
apple peeler
small knife
medium pie dish
tablespoon
baking sheet
oven gloves

This is an easy-to-make hot pudding
which is delicious served with custard,
cream, yogurt or ice-cream. You could
use other fruits instead of apples, such
as pears, pineapple or bananas. In the
autumn, try adding a handful or two of
blackberries to the apples.

*Apple crumble is a warming pudding,
particularly popular in autumn and winter.*

Apple crumble

1 Put the flour into the mixing bowl. Cut the butter or margarine into small chunks and add to the flour.

2 Using the tips of your fingers (which should be very well washed), rub the butter or margarine into the mixture, lifting your fingers up in the air and letting the flour fall down. This is known as 'rubbing-in'. Do this until the mixture looks like fine crumbs. Stir in half the caster sugar.

3 Peel the apples. Using a small knife, cut them into quarters, then carefully cut out the core. Chop the fruit up into small chunks.

4 Put the apple into a pie dish and sprinkle over the remaining caster sugar and the cinnamon. Splash about 5 tablespoons of water on top.

5 Sprinkle over the crumble mixture, spreading it evenly over the fruit. Sprinkle on the demerara sugar. Place the pie dish on a baking sheet.

6 Preheat the oven to 190°C, 375°F or gas mark 5. Bake the crumble for about 30 minutes until the topping is golden brown and the apples are bubbling underneath. Remove from the oven using oven gloves and cool the crumble before serving.

Strawberry and lemon whim-wham

Ingredients
Serves 6

300 ml whipping cream, or 150 ml cream and 150 g natural yogurt
grated rind of 1 large lemon
2 tablespoons caster sugar
6 sponge finger biscuits
250 g strawberries, sliced
a few almond flakes

Equipment

whisk
bowl
small knife and chopping board
fine grater
six glasses, e.g. wine glasses (the prettier the better)

This is a quick version of trifle. In the past, cooks would 'wham' in fruit and pieces of cake according to their 'whim'.

1   Whisk the cream with the lemon rind and sugar until fairly stiff. If you are using yogurt, whip the cream then fold in the yogurt.

2   Break up the biscuits and place in the base of the glasses. Scatter over the strawberries.

3   Spoon over the cream, decorate with almonds and chill in the fridge.

This trifle contains custard as well as cream.

Glossary

Batter A thick liquid made of flour, egg and milk. It is used for making pancakes and for coating food before frying.

Brandy A strong alcoholic drink.

Capital The main city of a country. The capital is usually the centre of government.

Casserole A kind of stew. The word refers to the pottery or glass dish, with a lid, in which the stew is cooked.

Christians People who follow a religion based on the teachings of Jesus Christ. Britain is a mostly Christian country. There are also Jews, Muslims, Hindus and Sikhs.

Cider An alcoholic drink made from apple juice.

Climate The kind of weather a place generally has.

Colander A big pan with holes in it for draining food.

Droughts Periods when there is little or no rain.

Dumplings Balls of sticky dough served with stews.

Efficient Working very well, with no wasted effort.

Empire A group of many countries all ruled under one person – the emperor.

Fasting Going without food.

Fertile When referring to soil, fertile means very rich and nourishing, thus encouraging plants to grow.

Fodder crops Crops such as hay or maize grown especially for feeding to animals.

Gravy A sauce made from the juices that come out of meat when it is cooking.

Graze To feed on the grass or other plants in a field.

Griddle A round iron hotplate used for cooking scones.

Herbs Plants with a delicious smell, used in cooking to flavour food.

Hothouse A building with a glass roof and walls in which the air can be kept quite hot.

Marmalade A kind of jam made from oranges.

Marzipan A paste made of ground almonds, sugar and egg whites. It is often spread over cakes.

Moors Large areas of land, usually covered in coarse grass and heather.

Multicultural Including the various traditions of people from many different races and backgrounds.

Offal The internal parts of an animal that can be eaten. For example, liver and kidneys are offal.

Pickles Vegetables which have been bottled in vinegar so that they can be kept without going rotten.

Preserve To prepare food so that it does not go off, for example by freezing, drying, salting or pickling.

Recipe A list of ingredients and instructions for making a dish of food.

Society The system of customs, traditions and organizations shared by one group of people.

Spices Substances, usually made from plants, with a strong taste and smell, used to give food a special flavour. For example, ginger and cinnamon are spices.

Spirits Strong alcoholic drinks such as brandy, whisky or gin.

Spit A rod used in the past for roasting meat. The meat was put on the rod, which could be turned slowly over a fire.

Staple Most important. A staple food is the food eaten as the main part of a person's diet, such as bread or rice.

Stock A tasty liquid made by boiling meat or fish bones and vegetables in water.

Stuffing A tasty mixture of chopped ingredients, such as breadcrumbs and herbs, stuffed inside a joint of meat before roasting.

Suet A special, very hard, animal fat.

Syrup A thick, sweet liquid made from sugar.

Traditional According to customs that have been handed down over the centuries.

Trend A general tendency.

Vanilla The pod or bean from the vanilla plant, which has a strong taste and is used to flavour food, especially sweet foods such as ice-cream.

Vegetarianism A system of eating which excludes all meat and fish.

Vinegar A sour-tasting liquid made from the alcohol in beer, wine or cider.

Whisky A strong alcoholic drink made from barley.

Worcestershire sauce A tangy, dark-brown liquid made from soya, vinegar and spices. Because it is strong, very little is needed to flavour food.

Further information

Information books

British Food and Drink by Anna Sproule (Wayland, 1988)

Great Britain by Anna Sproule (Wayland, 1988)

Inside Great Britain by Ian James (Franklin Watts, 1988)

Passport to Great Britain by Andrew Langley (Franklin Watts, new edition 1993)

The United Kingdom by David Flint (Simon and Schuster Young Books, 1992)

Recipe books

The Sainsbury Book of Children's Cookery by Roz Denny and Caroline Waldegrave (Sainsbury/ Walker Books, 1993)

Teachers' resource

Household Food Consumption and Expenditure (the report of the National Food Survey Committee in the UK, published annually by HMSO and available in public libraries)

Acknowledgements

The publishers would like to thank the following for allowing their photographs to be reproduced: Anthony Blake Photo Library 12 top (G. Buntrock), 21 bottom, 26 top, 34 top, 44; Bridgeman Art Library 14 (Christopher Wood Gallery, London); Cephas 4, 30 both; Chapel Studios 38, 40, 42 (all Z. Mukhida); Greg Evans International cover, 10 bottom (G. B. Evans), 11 bottom (A. Ramsay), 28 (G. B. Evans), 33 (G. B. Evans); Mary Evans 13, 15; Eye Ubiquitous 6 (J. Okwesa), 11 top (P. Thompson), 18 top (P. Thompson), 21 top (P. Seheult), 29, 31 bottom, 35; Chris Fairclough Colour Library 22; Fotomas Index 12 bottom; Tony Stone Worldwide frontispiece (E. Craddock), 7 (D. Muscroft), 18 bottom (J. Calder), 19 (S. Yeo), 23 (R. Weller), 24, 27 (A. Blake), 32, 34 bottom (S. and N. Geary); Topham 16 top, 25 bottom, 26 bottom, 31 top (M. Rodgers); Simon Warner 8 both; Wayland Picture Library cover inset (A. Blackburn), 9, 10 top, 16 bottom (M. Power), 17, 20 top (A. Hasson), 20 bottom; Zefa 25 top.

The map artwork on page 5 and graph artwork on page 17 was supplied by Peter Bull. The recipe artwork on pages 36-7, 39, 41, 43 and 44 was supplied by Judy Stevens.

Index